The Diane Bish Wedding Book

SERVICE MUSIC FOR ORGAN

Arrangements by
Diane Bish

GENTRY PUBLICATIONS

FOREWORD

Whenever I have played for a wedding, I must carry 37 books (at least) to the console in order to have all of the selections I want and need for the occasion. How often I have longed for a volume of music with "EVERYTHING YOU'VE ALWAYS WANTED TO PLAY FOR A WEDDING BUT NEVER COULD FIND." And so, here it is, a book with my favorite and most requested wedding music, all in one place. I have tried to edit the music as I like to play it, including registrations and manual changes. I suggest, however, that you adjust the marked registrations to fit the organ you play, the acoustics of the room, and the proper effect you are trying to create. Attempt always to be creative and interesting in your interpretation of the music.

I am hopeful you will find this book as handy as I have and that you will at last have a one music-book wedding and a tidy music rack.

Diane Bish

Diane Bish
Ft. Lauderdale, Florida, May 1980

This book is dedicated to Nell Wyman, my good friend and secretary of the music department of Coral Ridge Presbyterian Church, who, by keeping me organized, has made it possible for me to edit and compile this book. Thank you, Nell.

TABLE OF CONTENTS

COMPOSER INDEX

Psalm 19

Sw. Fondations 8' 4' 2', Mixtures, Sw. to Ch.
Ch. Fondations 8' 4' 2', Cymbals
Gt. Fondations 8' 4' 2', Mixtures
Ped. 16' 8' 4', Sw. to Ped.

Benedetto Marcello
Edited by Diane Bish

Gt.
Ch.
Gt.
l. h.
add Gt. Scharf
l. h.

add Sw. Trumpet
l.h.
broadly
add Sw. 16'4' reeds
fff
fff
rall.

Rondeau

Sw. Principals 8' 4' 2', Mixtures, Sw. to Ch.
Ch. Principals 8' 4' 2', Mixtures
Gt. Solo Trumpet
Ped. 16' 8' 4', Sw., Ch. to Ped.

Joseph Mouret
Edited by Diane Bish

add Sw. reeds 16'8'4'
Ch.
ff
Gt.
Sw. reeds off
Ch.
tr

add Sw. reeds 16'8'4'
Ch.
ff
tr
tr
tr
Sw.
Ch.
Sw. reeds off
Sw.
Ch.

add Sw. reeds 16'8'4'
Gt.
ff
Ch.
tr
tr
tr
cresc.
ritard.
tr

Wedding March

(Midsummer Night's Dream)

Sw. Principals, Mixtures, Reeds, 16' 8' 4', Sw. to Ch. Gt. 8'
Ch. Principals, Mixtures, Ch. to Gt.
Gt. Principals, Mixtures
Ped. 16' 8' 4', Sw., Ch. to Ped.

Felix Mendelssohn
Edited by Diane Bish

G-555

sf
sf
Gt.
tr
tr
1.
2.
all reeds, mixtures off
Ch.
mp
1.
2.
ff

Gt. ff
ff
add Sw. reeds 16'8'4'
ff
tr
3
tr
reeds
Sw.
p
Gt.
Sw.
p

sf
p
p
Ch.
cresc.
cresc.
molto cresc.
Ch.
p
cresc.
Gt.
cresc.

add Sw. reeds, mixtures
add Gt. mixtures
Gt. ff

tr
f
ff
1.
2.

Allegro Moderato

Sw. Principals, Flutes 8' 2', Sw. to Ch.
Ch. Principals, Flutes 8' 2',
Gt. Principals 8' 4' 2', Scharf Mixture
Ped. 16' 8' Sw. to Ped.

George F. Handel
Edited by Diane Bish

Gt. f
Ch.
Gt.

Now Thank We All Our God

(March Triomphale)

Sw. Full with reeds 16' 8' 4'
Sw. to Ch. 8' 4', Sw. to Gt.
Ch. Full Ch. to Gt. 8' 4'
Gt. Full with reeds
Ped. Full, Sw. Ch. Gt. to Ped.

Sigfried Karg-Elert
Edited by Diane Bish

Maestoso with Movement

The signs × and ⌐¬ indicate the thematic motives (the chorale melody as transformed rhythmically by augmentation or diminution).

*2nd time more ritard than first.

Sw. +Mix.
simile
p
Ch.
Gt.
cresc.
pp
rffs
fff
tr
Ped.
brillante
da capo
al Fine

In Thee is Gladness

Sw. Principals 8' 4' 2', Mixtures, Sw. to Gt.
Ch. Principals, Mixtures, Ch. to Gt.
Gt. Principals 8' 4' 2', Scharf Mixture
Ped. 16' 8' 4', Trumpet 16' 8' Sw., Gt. to Ped.

J. S. Bach
Edited by Diane Bish

Bright Allegro - detached

tr
(tr)
tr
tr
tr
tr
tr

Broaden Slightly

Pavane

Sw. Flutes, Strings, Trem., Sw. to Ch. 8'
Ch. Flutes, Strings, Trem.
Gt. Harmonic Flute 8' 4', Sw. Ch. to Gt. 8' 4'
Ped. Bourd 16', Ch. to Ped. 32'

Robert Elmore
Edited by Diane Bish

A tempo
soft strings
Gt.
Flute solo
Clar. solo
Freely
Clar.
Flute
Strings.
poco rall.
Sw.
a tempo
String 4'-16'
mp
Vox
Ch. Flutes 8'-4', Trem.
p Flutes

Tempo I
rall.
Sw.
Oboe trem.
mp
Ch. Strings
p
More slowly
8va
Erzahlers, trem.
p
pp
Fr. Horn.
p
add 32' untersatz

Adagio

Sw. Strings, Sw. to Gt.
Ch. Flutes 8' 4', Ch. to Gt.
Gt. Flutes 8' 4'
Ped. 16' 8', Sw. to Ped., Ch. to Ped.

Felix Mendelssohn
Edited by Diane Bish

Sw.
Ch.
Sw.
r.h.
l.h.
Ch.
Gt. mf
add Sw.
Flutes 8'4'
f
pp

Ch.
Gt.
Sw.
Ch.
Sw.
Sw.
Gt.
Ch.
pp
Sw.
pp

Hail This Brightest Day of Days

1 *
Sw. Principals, Mixtures, Sw. to Ch.
Ch. Principals, Mixtures
Gt. Solo Trumpet
Ped. 16' 8' 4', Sw. Ch. to Ped.
or
2 *
Sw. Principals 8' 4' 2', Sw. to Ch.
Ch. Principals 8' 4' 2'
Gt. Cornet
Ped. 16' 8' 4', Sw. Ch. to Ped.

J. S. Bach
Edited by Diane Bish

*Two registrations are possible.

Rigaudon

[1]
Sw. Full without reeds, Sw. to Ch., Gt. 8'
Ch. Full without reeds, Ch. to Gt.
Gt. Full without reeds
Ped. Full without reeds, 16' 8' 4' 32' prestant

[2]
Sw. Solo reed or reeds, 8' 4'
Ch. Principals 16' 8' 4' Ch. to Gt.
Gt. Principals 16' 8' 4'
Ped. 16' 8', Ch. to ped. Gt. to ped.

Andre Campra
Arranged by Diane Bish

Gt.
Sw.
add Sw. reeds 16'8'4'
fff

Broaden
2
Sw.
Gt.
Sw.
Gt.
Sw.
Tr.

2
add Sw. reeds 16'8'4'
Gt.
fff-sfz
rit.

Trumpet Tune in D

Sw. Principals 8' 4' 2', Mixtures, Sw. to Ch.
Ch. Principals 8' 4' 2', Mixtures
Gt. Solo Trumpet
Ped. 16' 8' 4', Sw. to Ped.

Henry Purcell
Edited by Diane Bish

Marcato, Stately, dignified

tr
tr
Sw. reed
16' off
Sw. reed
4' off
Sw. Trumpet
8' off
tr
tr

add Sw. reeds 16'8'4'
tr
cresc.
rit.

Hornpipe

Sw. 8' 2', Sw. to Ch. and Gt.
Ch. Flutes 8' 2'
Gt. 8' 4' 2', Mix.
Ped. 16' 8' Sw. to Ped.

George F. Handel
Edited by Diane Bish

Arioso in A
(Air on the G String)

Sw. Strings, Trem., Sw. to Sw. 16' 4', Sw. to Ch. 16' 8' 4'
Ch. Strings, Trem. Ch. to Ch. 4'
Gt. Flutes 8' 4', All to Gt. 16' 8' 4'
Ped. 16' 8' 32' Resultant

J. S. Bach
Edited by Diane Bish

Largo - very expressive

1.
2.
Ch.
mp
Sw.
tr
Gt.
Sw. Flute 8' off
Ch.
ten.
add Ch. 8'4' Flutes

Ch.
Sw. 8' Flute off
Ch. 8'4' Flute off
Sw.
tr
1.
2.
tr
ppp
ppp

Air I

Sw. Strings, Sw. to Sw. 4', Trem., Sw. to Ch.
Ch. Strings, Flutes 8'
Gt. Flutes, 8' 4'
Ped. 16' 8' Soft, Sw. to Ped.

George F. Handel
Edited by Diane Bish

Larghetto - expressive

cresc.
pp
Gt.
mf
p

a tempo
tr
rit.
Sw. Voix céleste
cresc.
Sw. to Sw. 4' off
dim.
tr
rall.
ppp
ppp

O Had I Jubal's Lyre

Sw. Oboes, Trem.
Ch. Flutes 8' 4', Ch. to Ped.
Gt. 8' 4' Flutes, 2 2/3' Trem.
Ped. 16' 8' Soft

George F. Handel
Edited by Diane Bish

Sw.
Gt.
tr
Sw.
tr

Trumpet Voluntary

Sw. Principals, Mixtures, Sw. to Ch. 8'
Ch. Principals, Mixtures
Gt. Solo Trumpet
Ped. 16' 8' Sw. Ch. to Ped.

Jeremiah Clark
Edited by Diane Bish

Maestoso with motion
solo Trumpet

tr
add Sw. reeds
Ch.
ff
Gt. solo Trumpet

tr
Ch. ff
tr
tr
tr
tr
solo Trumpet
f
Gt.
simile
Ch. ff

tr.
Gt. solo Trumpet
tr
f
Ch. add Sw. reeds
tr
tr
Full Organ tr
ff
Gt.
tr
tr
tr
tr
rit.

Air II

Sw. Oboes, 4' Flute, Trem.
Ch. Flute 8' (4')
Gt. Solo Flute
Ped. 16' 8', Ch. to Ped.

George F. Handel
Edited by Diane Bish

cresc.
mf
tr
Sw.
Gt.
Sw.

Sw. 8'4'2 2/3' Trem.
Ch. Strings
Gt.
tr.
mf
Sw.
mp
Ch.
Gt.

cresc.
mf
Sw.
Gt.
Sw.
Gt.
f
allargando
tr.

Allegro Maestoso

(Water Music)

Sw. Trumpet 8'
Ch. Principals 8' 4' 2', Mixtures, Ch. to Gt.
Gt. Principals, Mixtures
Ped. 16' 8', Ch. to Ped.

George F. Handel
Edited by Diane Bish

Gt.
mf
Sw.
f
mp
mf
Ch.
Gt.
rit.

Jesu, Joy of Man's Desiring

Sw. Strings, Trem., Sw. to Ch.
Ch. Strings, Trem. Ch. to Ch. 16' 4'
Gt. Flutes 8' 4'
Ped. Soft 16' 8' Sw. to Ped.

J. S. Bach
Edited by Diane Bish

Andante - flowing motion

Gt.
Ch.
Gt.
Ch.
Gt.
Gt.
Ch.
Ch.
Gt.
Gt.

Ch.
Ch.
Gt.
Gt.
add Ch. to Ch. 4'
add Gt. 2'
Ch.
Ch.

Gt.
Gt.
l.h.
Ch.
Ch.
Gt.
Gt.
Ch.
l.h.
Ch.
Gt.
Gt.
Ch.
Ch.

off Gt. 2'
Gt.
Gt.
off Gt. 4'
rit.
pp
pp

Allegretto

1
Sw. Principals, Mixtures, Sw. to Ch.
Ch. Principals, Mixtures
Gt. Solo Trumpet
Ped. 16' 8' Sw. to Ped.

2
Sw. 8' 4' Flutes, Sw. to Ch.
Ch. 8' 4' Flutes
Gt. 8' 2' Principals
Ped. 16' 8' Sw. to Ped.

George F. Handel
Edited by Diane Bish

tr
Fine
mp
rit. 2nd time
2
With more movement
Gt.
mf
Ch.

D. C. al Fine

Adagio Cantabile

(Violin Sonata No. 3)

Sw. Oboes, Trem.
Ch. Strings
Gt. 8' 4' 2 2/3' Flutes, Trem.
Ped. Soft 16' 8'

J. S. Bach
Edited by Diane Bish

Very expressive

Gt.
r.h. on Ch.
1.
rit.
2.
Gt.

Sw.
Gt.
tr
rall.
(solo)

Gavotte

Sw. Oboes
Ch. 8' 4' 2 2/3' 2'
Gt. 8' 4' 2', principal
Ped. 16' 8' 4' flutes

Samuel Wesley
Edited by Diane Bish

Sw.
mp
simile
tr
mp
Ch.
Gt. f
f
2nd time
ff e rall.
ff

Air

Sw. 8' 4' 2 2/3', Trem.
Ch. 8' Flute
Gt. 8' 4' Flutes, Trem.
Ped. 16' 8' soft

Samuel Wesley
Edited by Diane Bish

Sw.

Gt. add Gemshorn
tr
Broaden

Trumpet Allemande

Sw. Principals, Mixtures, reeds, 16' 8' 4', Sw. to Ch.
Ch. Principals, Mixtures
Gt. Solo Trumpet
Ped. 16' 8' 4' Sw. Ch. to Ped.

Anthony Holborne
Edited by Diane Bish

Maestoso - with dignity

*Solo may be played one octave lower.

tr
Ch.
ff
Gt.
Solo Trumpet
f
Ch.

Ch. ff

Gt.
optional Ped.
allargando
Gt.
ff Full Organ
ff
rit.

Thou Shalt Bring Them In

Sw. 4' 2 2/3', Trem.
Ch. Strings
Gt. Flute 8' 2', Trem.
Ped. 16' 8' Ch. to Ped.

George F. Handel
Edited by Diane Bish

Gt.
Sw.
tr
rit.

Bridal Chorus

(Lohengrin)

Sw. Principals, Flutes 8' 4', Sw. to Gt. 8', Sw. to Gt. 8'
Ch. Principals, Flutes 8' 4', Ch. to Gt. 8'
Gt. Principals, Flutes 8' 4' 2'
Ped. 16' 8' Sw. to Ped.

Richard Wagner
Edited by Diane Bish

*If the march has to be lengthened, as it so often is, repeat to this point from the 5th measure, and repeat as often as required.

Trumpet Tune and Air

[1]
Sw. Fondations 8' 4' 2', Mixtures Sw. to Ch. 8'
Ch. Fondations 8' 4' 2'
Gt. Solo Trumpet
Ped. 16' 8' 4' Sw., Ch. to Ped.

[2]
Ch. 8' 4' Flutes
Gt. 8' 2' 2 2/3'
Ped. Soft 16' 8', Ch. to Ped.

Henry Purcell
Edited by Diane Bish

[1] **Marcato - Maestoso with movement**

tr
Gt.
Ch.
Ch.

Fine
Gt. Solo reed, full organ
fff
2
Gt.
simile
Ch.
detached
1.
2.
D.C. al Fine